100 WRITING PROMPTS

EXPOSITORY WRITING PROMPTS

How to Use Writing Prompts	page 2
100 Writing Prompts	pages 3-102
Blank Writing Pages	pages 103-108
About the Author	page 109
MediaStream Press	page 110

COPYRIGHT & OTHER NOTES

All material and designs in this book are copyrighted (C) 2015 Andrew Frinkle. Graphics and cliparts are from openclipart.org or other royalty free sources.

You may make copies of the material within the book for personal and classroom use only. This is a single-teacher/user license.

It is suggested that you check the prompts you will use before using them with your children or students. Please remove any that you do not think are appropriate for the age level of the students or the setting. They are provided to be interesting writing experiences, but may not fit for all students and situations.

(C) 2015 MediaStream Press & Andrew Frinkle

HOW TO USE THESE WRITING PROMPTS

I. **QUICK WRITE**
   a. Select a single page (you can also just do them in order)
   b. Set a timer.
   c. Give students about 1 minute to brainstorm the topic.
   d. Set the timer again.
   e. Give students 2-10 minutes to write.
   f. Review results. These can also be used as a rough draft to practice editing and revision.

II. **RANDOM CHOICE**
   a. Have a stack of these pages ready to go, 1 per student.
   b. Students will choose one to write about.
   c. Set expectations (time, length, revision opportunities)
   d. Write!

III. **SWAP PASS MAYHEM**
   a. Students each choose a topic.
   b. Then, each student brainstorms for a few minutes and begins an essay.
   c. After a few minutes or writing, usually a set time like 5 minutes, call for a PASS! (It's best if you sit in teams of 3-4.)
   d. According to you, determine if students pass their essays left, right, front, back, or just around their tables. Spinners might help determine this, especially if you assign different numbers different directions.
   e. Give students a very brief brainstorming time to read and figure out how to add to the other student's essay.
   f. Students get more writing time then, until you are done or until you wish to call another pass, if you wish to repeat the previous steps.
   g. Afterward, it is encouraged to allow students to share their frustrations, amusements, and creative discoveries.

IV. **PARTNER WRITING**
   a. Give a pair of students 1 prompt.
   b. Students review and brainstorm for 1-2 minutes.
   c. Students the write their own essays.
   d. After a set amount of time, students swap papers and edit what their partner has written.
   e. Swap back for revisions.

V. **ALTERNATE ENDINGS**
   a. Choose a prompt.
   b. Show the whole class which prompt was chosen and then discuss some ideas.
   c. Together, the class begins an essay and takes turns adding on a few small parts up until things get interesting…
   d. Students then have to finish the essays on their own.
   e. You might wish to share results or discuss final products later.

My Favorite Thing

Write about your favorite thing.

Animals Two-By-Two

Compare and contrast two animals.

If I Had $$$

Write about what you would do if you found $100 or $1000 dollars.

My Favorite Game

Write about your favorite sport or game.

The Best Day Ever

Write about the best day you ever had.

Hobbies

Write about a hobby you have.

My Favorite Person

Write about your favorite person.

Natural Disasters

Write about one or more natural disasters, like: hurricanes, tornados, mudslides, earthquakes, floods, etc...

Best Show Ever

Describe your favorite TV show or movie and explain why it is the best one ever.

Experimental

Write about a science project or activity you have done. What happened? What did you learn?

The Worst Day Ever

Write about the worst day you ever had.

My Family

Describe your family.

Free Time

Write about what you would do tomorrow if you had the day off and could do anything.

My Hero

Write about someone you consider to be a hero.

Best Present

Describe your favorite present you have ever received.

A Scary Thing Happened...

Explain a scary situation you have experienced.

Uniformity

If you have school uniforms, what do you like or not like about them? If you don't, would you like to? Why?

Super Powers

Write about a super power you wish you had and how you would use it.

Tough Choices

Write about a time when you had to make a difficult decision.

Inspirational

Write about something that inspires you.

When I Grow Up

Write about what you want to be when you grow up.

Best Teacher Ever

Write about a teacher that you really like or liked. Why were they so great?

Hard Times

Write about something that was difficult for you.

Better to Give...

Write about a time when you gave someone a gift. How did it make you feel?

Seasons

Explain why you like one season more than the others.

Something New

Write about something new you have recently learned.

Most Important Thing Said to Me

Write about the most important thing or piece of advise someone ever said to you.

First Time

Write about something you did for the first time.

Extinction

Write about an endangered or extinct animal.

Pets

Write about the pet you have or wish you have.

Do-Overs

Write about something you wish you could do over or try again.

Creepy Crawlies

Write about a creature or animal you think is really gross.

Principal for the Day

Describe what you would do if you were principal of the school for the day.

Perfect Job

Write about your dream job.

Color Feelings

Describe how different colors (or shapes and textures) make you feel.

Best Song Ever

Describe your favorite singer and explain why they are the best one ever. You can also write about the best song ever, instead of the singer.

Important

Write about something that it is important to do.

Meet and Greet

Write about someone you really want to meet in person.

Outer Space

Write about astronauts and space. What do you know?

Happy Place

Describe a place that makes you feel happy and why it makes you feel that way.

Collectors

Write about something you collect and why you collect them.

Birthday Cheer

Write about the best birthday you ever had.

Coolest Toy Ever

Write about a favorite toy you had when you were a young child.

In Sickness & Health

Write about a time when you or a family member was sick.

Recipes

Explain how to cook or prepare a food item you can make.

BFF's

Explain why someone is your best friend.

Complete Characters

Which movie, tv show, or story character would you like to be? Why?

Herb Culture

Describe a plant. What is it used for? Where does it grow?

100 WRITING PROMPTS

Game Changers

Write about how something or someone changed your life.

Zoo Time

Write about a type of animal that you like or find interesting.

Goals

Write about a goal you have set for yourself. Have you accomplished it? If not, how will you pursue that goal?

Vacation Fever

Write about the best vacation you've ever been on.

Last Time

Write about something you never want to do again.

Good Feelings

Write about several things that make you feel good. Why do they make you feel that way?

Sightseeing

Write about something you want to see or a place you want to visit.

Discoveries

Write about what you think is the MOST important scientific/technological discover ever.

Schedules

Explain your daily routine and schedule.

Similar Characters

Compare and contrast 2 characters from similar stories.

Procedure Writing

Explain a process or procedure step-by-step.

Inedible

Describe a food you just can't eat and why you can't eat it.

Manimals

If you could be any animal in the world, what kind of animal would you be? Why? How would your life change?

Forgotten

Write about a time when you forgot something important. What happened because of it?

New Thrills

Write about an activity you want to try or an event you want to attend. It must be something you've not done or gone to before.

Biography

Write a biography of someone you know (not yourself).

Autobiography

Write your own biography.

Not That Again!

Write about something you really don't like to do, but sometimes have to. Explain why it is unpleasant for you.

Chores

Explain what chores and duties you have around the house.

In Hot Water

Write about a time you got in trouble. Explain why you got in trouble.

Siblings

Write about a brother or sister. If you don't have any siblings, write about which one you wish you had.

Spring

Write about Easter, a Spring festival, or what Spring means to you.

Summer

Write about the 4th of July, a Summer festival, or what Summer means to you.

Fall

Write about Thanksgiving, Halloween, a Fall/Harvest festival, or what Fall means to you.

Winter

Write about Christmas, a Winter festival, or what Winter means to you.

Friendship Shakeup

Write about a time when you argued with a friend. What happened? Why?

Best Sport Ever

Explain why the sport you play or like is the BEST one.

False Expectations

Write about a time when you were excited by something, only to be let down when you actually got it or experienced it.

Sequels

Compare and contrast a book or movie and its sequel.

Alternate Endings

Write about a story or movie's ending, proposing changes to the ending that could improve upon it.

Critique

Compare a book to an alternate form, like a movie, comic book adaptation, or tv show.

Technicalities

Write about technology and how you use it in your life every day.

Fashion Tragedy

Write about an outfit or piece of clothing that you wore that was just plain hideous. What's the ugliest thing you've ever worn?

Costumes

Describe your Halloween costume or a costume you wore for a different occasion. What makes or made it so great?

Lost in Space

Write about a time when you got lost or couldn't find something.

School Success

Explain how to be successful at school.

Determination

Describe a time when hard work and determination paid off for you or someone you know.

Admiration

Explain why you admire someone you know. Why are they worthy of admiration? What did they do? How do they act?

Bad Weather

Describe a time when you experienced bad weather. How did you feel? What happened?

Stories Happen

Describe a cause and effect in a story. What happened and why did it happen? What were the results?

Travel Time

Describe your first time on a boat, train, plane, or other mode of transportation.

Historical Figures

Write about a historical figure. What do you know about them? When and where did they live? What did they do?

Motivations

Write about a character in a movie, story, or TV show. Describe their motivations. Why do they do what they do?

A Better Place

What is one thing you can do to help make the world a better place? Explain with details.

Hard Work

Write about a job or profession. What is it like? How do you do that job?

Great Subject

Write about your favorite subject at school. Why do you like it?

Character Study

Compare yourself to a character in a movie, TV show, or book.

Places

Describe a place in detail.

Things

Describe an object in detail.

Life Happens

Describe a cause and effect in your life. What happened and why did it happen? What were the results?

Growing Up

Compare yourself now to a younger version of yourself.

A Different Era

If you could live in a different time in history, when would you want to live? Why?

WRITING & REVISION PAGE

… WRITING & REVISION PAGE …

100 WRITING PROMPTS
WRITING & REVISION PAGE

WRITING & REVISION PAGE

WRITING & REVISION PAGE

WRITING & REVISION PAGE

ANDREW FRINKLE

Andrew Frinkle is an award-nominated teacher and writer with experience in America and overseas, as well as years developing educational materials for big name educational sites like Have Fun Teaching. He has taught PreK all the way up to adult classes, and has focused on ESOL and EFL techniques. With a young child at home now, he's been developing more and more teaching strategies and books aimed at helping young learners.

His many educational works include:

- 50 STEM Labs, 50 More STEM Labs, 50 New STEM Labs, 50 STEM Labs Cards, & 50 Science Labs
- Common Core Assessment Templates
- Common Core Vocabulary Cards
- Elementary & Middle School Common Core Workbooks
- Graph Paper Math
- How to Draw with Basic Shapes
- Science Now!
- Sentence Builders & Word Builders
- Weekly Sentence Strips
- Story Starters
- Movers and Shakers Card Game & Expansion Sets
- Basic Skills Workbooks: Alphabet Skills, Colors, Number Sense, Nursery Rhymes, Phonics, and Shapes
- Sight Words Hopscotch Series
- Monster Zoo Math
- Dealing With Archetypical Children - A Classroom Management Resource
- Make Your Own Comic Books
- Board Game in a Book Series & Card Game in a Book Series
- Get this and other books on Amazon, Lulu, and other online booksellers!

Andrew Frinkle is the founder & owner of MediaStream Press LLC, which maintains the educational websites: www.littlelearninglabs.com, www.50STEMLabs.com, and www.common-core-assessments.com. He also writes fantasy and science fiction novels under the pen name Velerion Damarke. Read more at www.underspace.org

MEDIASTREAM PRESS

MediaStream Press offers over 60 fun and innovative books and games to help educate. Learn more at www.MediaStreamPress.com or search for buy directly at www.amazon.com/author/andrewfrinkle.

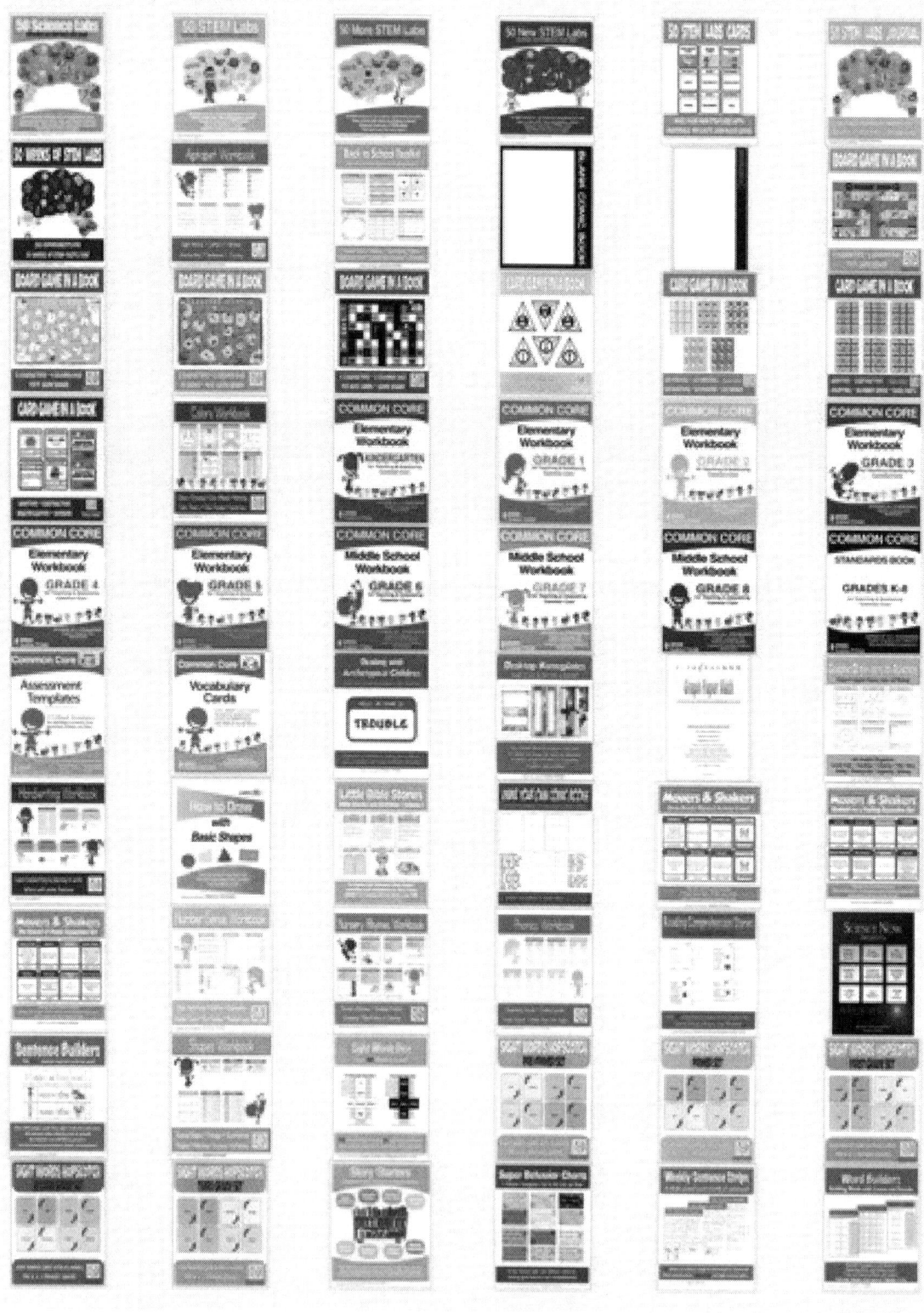

Made in the USA
Middletown, DE
26 April 2018